# See Under the Ocean

By Peter J

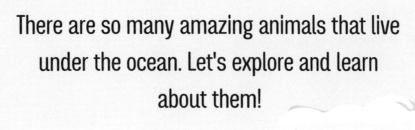

There are so many amazing animals that live
under the ocean. Let's explore and learn
about them!

Fish come in all different colors, shapes, and sizes. Clownfish are bright orange and have white stripes. They live in sea anemones.

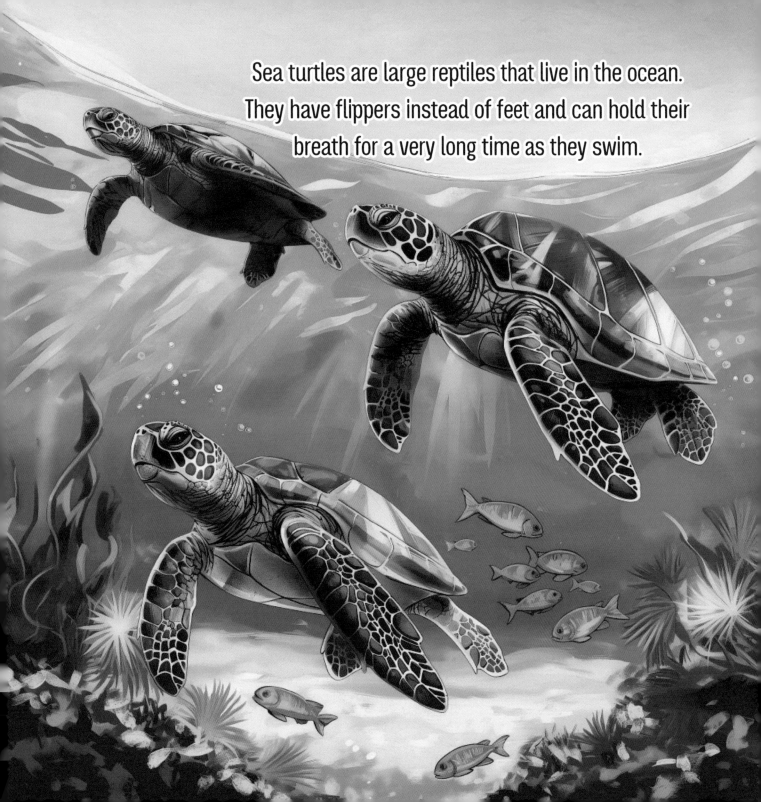

Sea turtles are large reptiles that live in the ocean. They have flippers instead of feet and can hold their breath for a very long time as they swim.

The crown-of-thorns starfish has sharp, poisonous spikes. It uses tiny tube feet to eat coral.

Octopuses and squids can change their skin color and feel to blend in and hide from danger. They are super soft, which lets them wiggle into really small spots.

Jellyfish pulse through the water, almost like they are dancing. Their bodies are made mostly of water with just a little bit of squishy material.

The blue whale is the biggest animal in the world.
These friendly giants can be longer than 100 feet,
which is as long as a basketball court from one end
to the other!

Sea otters float on their backs in the water, using their bellies as tables to hold their food, like crabs and mussels, while they eat.

Coral polyps are small creatures that create coral reefs. They live together in big, colorful groups called colonies, and there are millions of them!

Seahorses wrap their tails around sea grasses and corals so they don't drift away as they sleep.

The ocean can have huge waves and powerful water streams. When there's a storm, the waves can get as tall as houses!

Giant clams are big and colorful, like painted rocks on the ocean floor. They can live for more than 100 years, which is really old!

Moray eels, snake-like and living in reef cracks, breathe by opening their mouths. They have sharp teeth for catching fish and can swim in any direction.

Flashlight fish have shiny spots near their eyes that light up. They use these lights to see food and find their friends in the dark.

Anglerfish have a special glowing stick on their heads that looks like a fishing pole with a light. They use it to attract and catch their food.

Glow-in-the-dark-sharks like a night light, in green or blue colors. This is because they have tiny glowing bits in their skin.

The Mariana Trench is the deepest part of the ocean, more than 35,000 feet down. Imagine stacking a really tall building on top of another; that's how deep it is!

Whales, dolphins, and porpoises are sea animals that breathe air through special holes on top of their headsWhales, dolphins, and porpoises are sea when they come up to the water's surface.

Walruses have special whiskers to help them find food on the ocean bottom, and they use their big teeth to pull out yummy clams to eat.

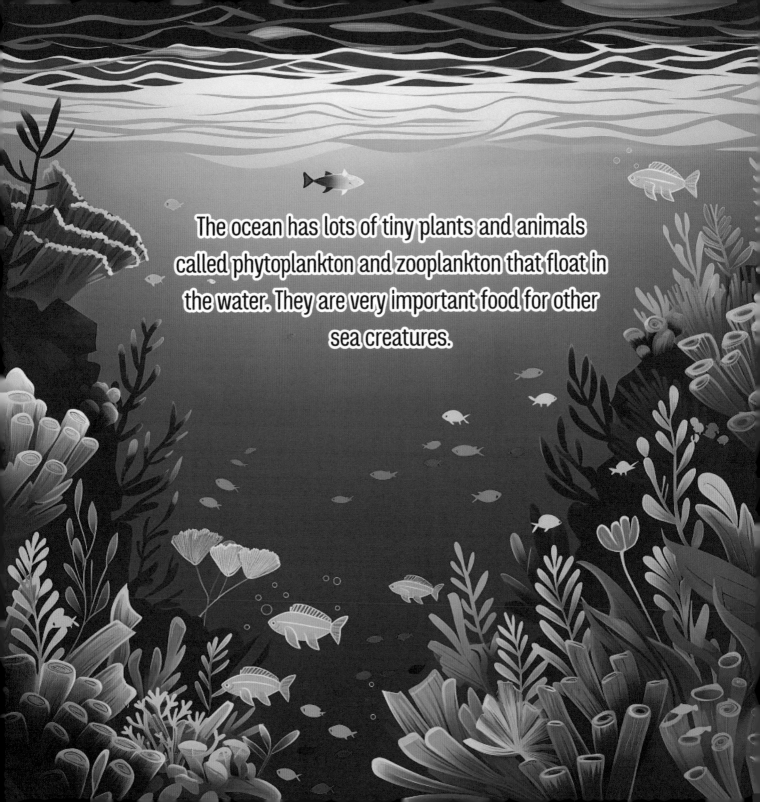

The ocean has lots of tiny plants and animals called phytoplankton and zooplankton that float in the water. They are very important food for other sea creatures.

Coral reefs are sometimes called "rainforests of the sea" because over 25% of marine life depends on them.

Parrot fish munch on coral all day and poop out fine white sand. Their poop helps create sandy beaches!

Isopods are tiny sea bugs that eat dead plants and animals on the ocean floor. Some of them even munch on wood that drops into the water!

Nudibranchs are colorful sea snails without shells. Their bright colors tell other animals they don't taste good!

Vampire squids are dark blue and have a cape-like skin. If they feel scared, they cover themselves with it like hiding under a blanket.

When scared, sea cucumbers throw up some of their insides to frighten or gross out enemies and get away.

Bobtail squids shoot out ink clouds to trick their enemies and quickly escape by using a special tube in their bodies.

Sharks can sense electric signals from the muscles and hearts of the animals they hunt. This helps them find food in dark or muddy water.

Starfish have 5 arms. They move using tube feet under their arms. They have tiny eyes to see all around.

Stingrays are flat fish that hide in the sand. They have long tails with a sting to keep safe from danger.

Spider crabs help keep the ocean clean by eating dead stuff off the seafloor. They're like the ocean's recycling team!

Lobsters have tough shells and big claws for defense and hunting. They walk with 8 legs and can regrow lost claws. They hide in caves by day and eat seafood and plants at night.

Pufferfish puff up like balloons when scared, have spiky skin, and use their fins to swim. They eat clams and mussels with their strong beaks.

Lionfish have zebra stripes and spiky fins that can sting. They eat small fish quickly and are very fast swimmers. They look fancy!

Dugongs, called sea cows, eat sea grass in shallow waters. They can stay underwater for 6 minutes and breathe through head nostrils. Baby dugongs drink their mom's milk.

Flying fish glide in the air with big fins to escape predators. They have sleek, torpedo-shaped bodies for speed and use their tails to launch out of the water.

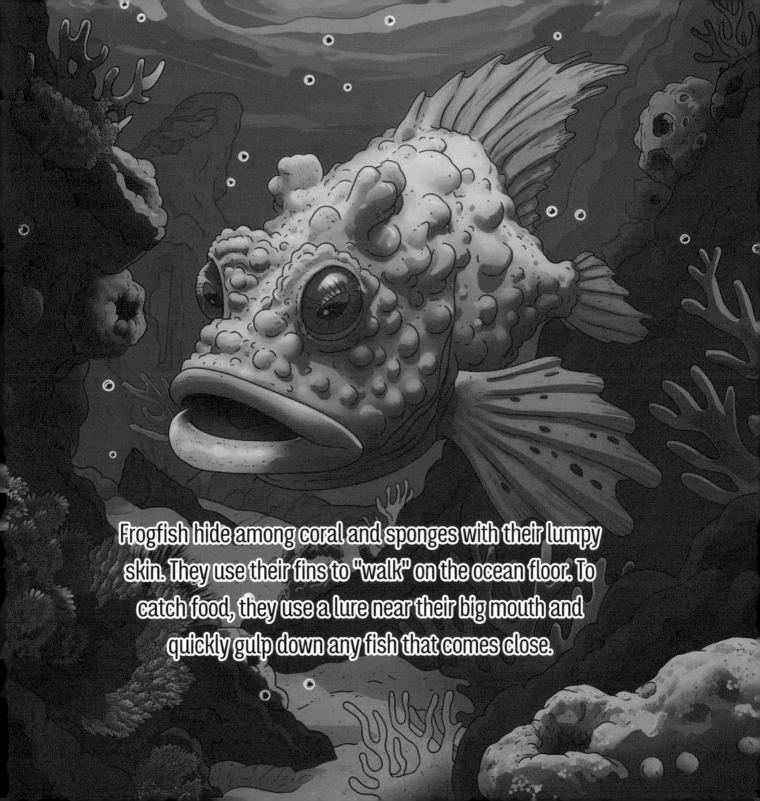

Frogfish hide among coral and sponges with their lumpy skin. They use their fins to "walk" on the ocean floor. To catch food, they use a lure near their big mouth and quickly gulp down any fish that comes close.

Narwhals have long, spiraled "horns" for hunting under the ice. They communicate with clicks and live in the Arctic, near Canada and Greenland. They're the sea's unicorns!

Mantis shrimp are rainbow-colored and have big claws. They see lots of colors and punch their food super fast. They live in warm oceans, hiding in sand and rocks. They're really cool

Sea dragons look like seaweed and eat tiny shrimp. There are leafy ones with lots of fins and weedy ones with bumps. Dad sea dragons carry the eggs until they hatch.

Tuna are fast, sleek fish that swim in groups in warm oceans. The biggest kind, the bluefin, can grow as big as a car. Baby tuna grow quickly but must watch out for predators.

There are so many more incredible animals under the ocean! Our mysterious seas still hold many surprises. Let's keep exploring!

## By the same author: Peter J
## Already published:

Printed in Great Britain
by Amazon

41897578R00027